Google Sheets Tutorial Guide

The Definitive User Manual To Master Sheets with Illustrations

By

Isaac Alejo

Table of Contents

INTRODUCTION

Google Sheets is a cloud-based spreadsheet software that has gained tremendous popularity within the business, academic, and personal spheres. Its user-friendly interface and robust capabilities empower users to structure, scrutinize, and visualize data in novel ways that the conventional spreadsheet approach couldn't offer.

One of the standout strengths of Google Sheets is its seamless fusion with other Google applications, like Google Drive, Google Docs, and Google Forms. This synergy enables effortless collaboration and sharing, making it a go-to tool for group projects and overseeing tasks.

We'll guide you through the diverse functionalities and potential of Google Sheets. Regardless of your skill level, you'll dive into crafting, refining, and styling spreadsheets and even harness formulas and functions for intricate calculations. Our coverage extends to advanced subjects such as data analysis, automation, and representation, propelling your data manipulation prowess.

However, this guide is wider than just the technical dimensions of Sheets. We'll also unveil how you can harness its capabilities to tackle real-world problems and enhance efficiency. You'll uncover the art of designing budget trackers, project management aids, and even uncomplicated games through Sheets.

As we journey through this guide, expect hands-on instances and clear step-by-step directives to aid you in mastering Sheets. You'll also gather insights, tips, and strategies for elevating your effectiveness. By the end, you'll wield a profound comprehension of Google Sheets and its potential to reshape your data interactions.

So, whether you're a business leader aiming to streamline your operations, a student seeking to excel in assignments, or an individual striving to bring order to personal finances, this guide caters to you. Let's embark on this exploration of Google Sheets and unleash its complete prowess.

Chapter 1: Google Sheets 101—The Beginner's Guide to Spreadsheets

While humans excel at processing visuals, forming word and concept associations, and retaining obscure facts, our capacity for mentally handling and storing precise, user-friendly datasets needs to be improved.

To address this, Data Tables—widely recognized as spreadsheets today—were devised to structure data sets that elude our memory. Spreadsheets enable us to arrange and categorize data logically, facilitating future reference and calculations.

The origins of this practice reach back thousands of years to the era of papyrus spreadsheets recorded in the journal of Merrer, an official during Egypt's Old Kingdom involved in constructing the Great Pyramid of Khufu.

In that era, paper was the primary medium for cataloging extensive data. However, the present era benefits from computer technology, relieving us of manual labor.

The debut of VisiCalc in 1979 marked the first digital spreadsheet, obviating the need for manual data entry, value calculations, and paper storage. As software progressed, programs like Excel, reigning as the most prominent spreadsheet software over the past three decades, propelled digital spreadsheets to the forefront of computing.

A single predicament persisted: these spreadsheets were bound to individual machines, complicating data sharing. Moreover, accidental deletion or computer crashes meant permanent loss of data.

Thus, Google's innovation in 2006 brought spreadsheets into the online realm through the Google Docs suite, advancing from the papyrus scratchpad's evolution. Google Sheets, the contemporary version, empowers collaborative online spreadsheet creation and number crunching across any internet-connected device.

- Google Sheets serves as an amped-up spreadsheet application. Resembling traditional tools, it gains immense potency as an online application. Key attributes include:

- Web-based functionality accessible anywhere, preventing forgotten files.

- Compatibility across devices, including iOS and Android mobile apps and web-based core applications.

- Google Sheets is free and bundles with Google Drive, Docs, and Slides, facilitating the online sharing of files, documents, and presentations.

- It encompasses nearly all the same functions as other spreadsheet software, making it familiar to Excel users.

- You can download additional tools, create your own, and even write custom code.

- Since it operates online, you can automatically collect data with your spreadsheet and perform various actions, even when it is closed.

Whether you're a newcomer to spreadsheets or an experienced Excel user seeking improved collaboration methods, this guide will assist you in maximizing your use of Google Sheets. We'll commence with foundational concepts in this chapter and proceed to explore advanced features, discover top add-ons, and instruct you on crafting your solutions.

Getting Started with Google Sheets

The optimal approach to mastering a tool like Sheets is to directly immerse yourself. Within this chapter, you'll acquire the skills to:

- Generate a Spreadsheet and Populate it with Information

- Arrange Data for Simple Visualization

- Apply Formulas to Add, Calculate Averages, and Filter Data

- Collaborate on, Safeguard, and Relocate Your Data

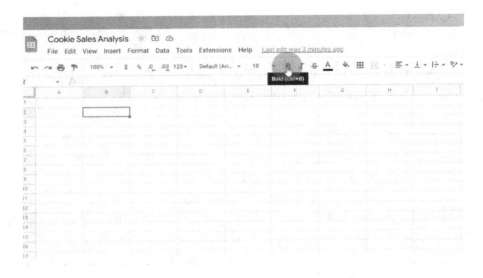

Common Spreadsheet Terms

To commence, let's familiarize ourselves with some spreadsheet terminology to aid your comprehension of the terms used in this guide:

- **Cell:** An individual data unit within a spreadsheet.

- **Column:** A vertical sequence of cells.

- **Row:** A horizontal sequence of cells.

- **Range:** A collection of cells spanning a row, column, or both.

- **Function:** An in-built operation within the spreadsheet application, employed for calculations involving cells, rows, columns, ranges, data manipulation, and more.

- **Formula:** The amalgamation of functions, cells, rows, columns, and ranges that yield a specific outcome.

- **Worksheet (Sheet):** Named assemblies of rows and columns comprising your spreadsheet; multiple sheets can exist within a single spreadsheet.

- **Spreadsheet:** The comprehensive document housing your worksheets.

If you're new to Google Sheets, or particularly if you're unfamiliar with spreadsheets altogether, look at Google's Getting Started Guide for Sheets. Additionally, it might be beneficial to bookmark Google's list of spreadsheet functions as a handy reference.

With this knowledge in mind, let's begin constructing our spreadsheets.

Create a Spreadsheet and Fill It With Data

A standout feature of Google Sheets lies in its free accessibility across all devices, facilitating seamless engagement with the tutorials in this guide. You only require a web browser, the Google Sheets app on your iOS or Android device, and a no-cost Google account. You're primed to begin by visiting sheets.google.com on your Mac or PC.

There exist three methods for initiating a new spreadsheet in Google Sheets:

- Click the red "NEW" button on your Google Drive dashboard and opt for "Google Sheets."

- Within an existing spreadsheet, access the menu and choose "File > New Spreadsheet."

- Click "Blank" or select a template on the Google Sheets homepage.

- This action generates a fresh, empty spreadsheet (or a template with pre-loaded content if preferred). However, for this tutorial, initiating with a blank spreadsheet is recommended.

The Google Sheets interface should resonate with at least one other spreadsheet application you've encountered, featuring recognizable text editing icons and tabs for additional sheets.

The sole divergence is that Google has streamlined the interface by minimizing clutter and displaying elements. Your initial task is self-evident: Integrate some data!

Several images within this chapter are dynamic animations. For the original GIFs, consult the online version of this chapter.

Adding Data to Your Spreadsheet

Survey the white-and-grey grid dominating your screen, and your immediate observation will likely be the blue border encircling the presently chosen cell or cells.

Upon opening a fresh spreadsheet, you'll observe that typing instantly populates the selected cell, usually in the upper-left corner. There is no need to double-click for input and minimal reliance on your mouse.

- **Insight:** A singular box within a spreadsheet goes by the name of a cell. Arranged into rows and columns with numerical and alphabetical labels, each cell accommodates a single value, term, or data fragment.

Feel free to pick any cell and proceed to input content. After entering data into a cell, you can choose from four options:

- Press ENTER to save and shift to the start of the subsequent row.

- Press TAB to save and progress rightward in the same row.

- Employ the ARROW KEYS (up, down, left, and right) on your keyboard to navigate one cell in the chosen direction.

- Click any cell to jump to it directly.

- If manual input feels cumbersome, there are alternative approaches for introducing data en masse:

- Copy and paste a list of text or numbers into your spreadsheet.

- Copy and paste an HTML table from a website.

- Import an existing spreadsheet in formats like csv, xls, or xlsx.

- Copy a value in one cell across a range of cells by clicking and dragging.

- While Copy & Paste is intuitive, scenarios may arise where attempting to copy spreadsheet-like data from a webpage or PDF results in either pasting everything into a single cell or preserving the original styling.

- Seek out data organized in an HTML table format (such as movie data from IMDB) to avoid encountering oddly pasted content in your spreadsheet.

- Ensure you single-click a cell before pasting data so Google Sheets arranges it as a list with each item in its cell. Double-clicking will likely combine all data into a single cell, which is often undesirable.

- If you encounter oddly formatted data, don't fret— resolution awaits in the following section!

- Importing files is equally straightforward. Choose to import directly into the present spreadsheet, create a new one, or replace a specific sheet (tab) with imported content.

- Commonly imported formats are CSV (comma-separated values), XLS, and XLSX (Microsoft Excel files). To import external files, navigate to FILE > IMPORT > UPLOAD.

Alternatively, if a Google Sheet (or a spreadsheet file like CSV, XLS, etc.) resides in your Google Drive, the same process applies for direct import into your spreadsheet—search your Drive from the import window.

Understanding how to duplicate a cell value warrants elaboration, as this action becomes pivotal once formulas populate your spreadsheets.

Utilizing the small blue dot in the lower-right corner of a selected cell and dragging it across or downward within a cell range offers various functionalities.

Multiple applications are possible with this feature:

- Replicating a cell's data into adjacent cells (while preserving formatting).

- Propagating a cell's "Formula" to nearby cells (a more advanced feature we will delve into later).

- Establishing an organized list of textual data.

The Google Sheets interface

To utilize and modify spreadsheets, it's necessary to become acquainted with the interface of Google Sheets.

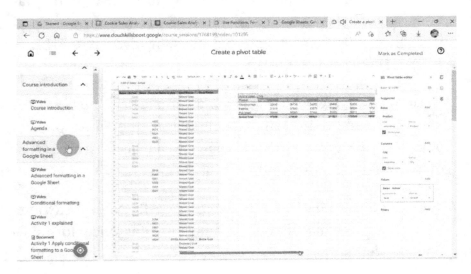

- **Spreadsheet Title:** Initially, a newly created spreadsheet is labeled as Untitled Spreadsheet. To change the name of the spreadsheet, click on its title.

- **Notification for Saved Changes:** Google Sheets automatically saves your modifications while you work. The notification for saved changes informs you that your spreadsheet has been saved.

- **Accessing Google Sheets Home Screen:** Click on this icon to return to your Google Sheets homepage.

- **Toolbar Menu:** Utilize the options in the toolbar menu to make various edits and adjustments to your spreadsheet. Click on a menu and pick the desired action from the drop-down list.

- **Collaboration Choices:** Collaboration options permit you to share your spreadsheet with others and provide comments while you work.

- **Shortcut Toolbar:** This toolbar supplies convenient shortcut buttons to format your spreadsheet's data, such as font size, text alignment, and text color.

- **Formula Bar:** The formula bar is used to input and modify data, functions, and formulas for a specific cell.

- **Column:** A column comprises cells arranged vertically from top to bottom. Columns are designated by letters. In this instance, Column C is chosen.

- **Cell:** Each rectangular section in a spreadsheet is called a cell. It marks the intersection of a row and a column. Click to choose a cell. In this example, Cell A1 is chosen.

- **Row:** A row encompasses cells running horizontally from side to side. Rows are identified by numbers. In this example, Row 9 is selected.

- **Sheets Toolbar:** Each spreadsheet can consist of multiple sheets. Click on the sheet tabs to switch between sheets and utilize the plus sign (+) to append a new sheet.

Cell basics

Each spreadsheet comprises numerous rectangles referred to as cells, where each cell represents the intersection of a row and a column. Columns are denoted by letters (A, B, C), and rows are identified by numbers (1, 2, 3).

For instance, the cell labeled as C10, in this case, signifies the intersection of column C and row 10.

Each cell has its unique identifier, known as a cell address, determined by its column and row. In the given example, the cell's address is C10.

When a cell is selected, its column and row headings become more prominent.

Moreover, you can select multiple cells together, forming a cell range. Instead of a single cell address, a cell range is indicated by the cell address of the first and last cells in the range, separated by a colon. For instance, a cell range containing cells A1, A2, A3, A4, and A5 would be represented as A1:A5.

In the provided images, two distinct cell ranges have been chosen:

- Cell range A2:A8

- Cell range A2:B8

Types of Cell References

Two categories of cell references exist: relative and absolute. These two types display varying behavior when transferred to different cells. Relative references alter as formulas are copied to new cells, whereas absolute references maintain constancy regardless of the copying location.

Relative references

By default, cell references are considered relative references. When duplicated across multiple cells, their adjustments are determined by the relative arrangement of rows and columns. For instance, duplicating the formula =A1+B1 from the first to the second row will transform into =A2+B2. Relative references prove particularly useful when replicating the same computation across numerous rows or columns.

How to create and copy a formula using relative references

For example, let's say our objective is to formulate a calculation that multiplies the price of each item by its corresponding quantity. Rather than generating distinct formulas for each row, a more efficient approach involves crafting a solitary formula in cell D4 and replicating it across other rows. To ensure accurate computations for each item, we will employ relative references.

Here's a step-by-step guide:

1. Choose the cell where you intend to insert the formula.

	A	B	C	D	E
1					
2	Food item	Unit price	Quantity	Line Total	
3	Beef picadillo	$2.99	15		
4	Chipotle shrimp	$3.99	10		
5	Carnitas	$2.89	10		
6	Vegetables	$2.29	30		
7	Chicken tings	$2.29	20		
8			Total	$0.00	
9					
10					
11					
12					

2. Input the formula to compute the desired outcome.

	A	B	C	D	E
1					
2	Food item	Unit price	Quantity	Line Total	
3	Beef picadillo	$2.99	15	=B3*C3	
4	Chipotle shrimp	$3.99	10		
5	Carnitas	$2.89	10		
6	Vegetables	$2.29	30		
7	Chicken tings	$2.29	20		
8			Total	$0.00	
9					
10					
11					

3. Confirm your entry by pressing the Enter key. The formula will be processed, and the outcome will be visible in the cell.

4. Opt for the cell you wish to duplicate. In our case, we'll select cell D4. The fill handle will become visible in the bottom-right corner of the cell.

	A	B	C	D	E
1					
2	Food item	Unit price	Quantity	Line Total	
3	Beef picadillo	$2.99	15	$44.85	
4	Chipotle shrimp	$3.99	10		
5	Carnitas	$2.89	10		
6	Vegetables	$2.29	30		
7	Chicken tings	$2.29	20		
8			Total	$44.85	
9					
10					
11					
12					
13					
14					

5. Click and drag the fill handle across the cells you want to populate.

	A	B	C	D	E
1					
2	Food item	Unit price	Quantity	Line Total	
3	Beef picadillo	$2.99	15	$44.85	
4	Chipotle shrimp	$3.99	10		
5	Carnitas	$2.89	10		
6	Vegetables	$2.29	30		
7	Chicken tings	$2.29	20		
8			Total	$44.85	
9					
10					

6. Release the mouse button. The formula will be duplicated into the chosen cells with relative references, and the outcomes will appear in each cell.

	A	B	C	D
1				
2	Food item	Unit price	Quantity	Line Total
3	Beef picadillo	$2.99	15	$44.85
4	Chipotle shrimp	$3.99	10	$39.90
5	Carnitas	$2.89	10	$28.90
6	Vegetables	$2.29	30	$68.70
7	Chicken tings	$2.29	20	$45.80
8			Total	$90.65
9				
10				
11				

For precision, you can double-click the populated cells to examine their formulas. The relative cell references should differ for each cell, varying according to their respective rows.

Absolute references

Begin by selecting the cell where the formula will reside. Input the formula to determine the desired value, like =(B4C4)E2, establishing E2 as an absolute reference. The formula will execute after pressing Enter, and the outcome will emerge in the cell.

Next, choose the cell you wish to duplicate. The fill handle will emerge in the lower-right corner of the cell. Drag the fill handle across the intended cells for filling, such as D5:D13, in our scenario. Upon releasing the mouse, the formula will be replicated to the selected cells with an absolute reference, thereby computing values for each cell.

You can double-click the populated cells to inspect their formulas for accuracy verification. The absolute reference should remain uniform across cells, while other references adapt relative to the cell's row.

Remember to insert the dollar sign ($) whenever establishing an absolute reference across multiple cells. Without the dollar sign, Google Sheets will interpret it as a relative reference, generating an erroneous outcome upon duplication to other cells.

How to create and copy formulas using absolute references

1. Choose the cell where you want the formula.

	A	B	C	D	E	F
1				TAX RATE:	7.50%	
2	Food item	Unit price	Quantity	Sales Tax	Line Total	
3	Beef picadillo	$2.99	15		$44.85	
4	Chipotle shrimp	$3.99	10		$39.90	
5	Carnitas	$2.89	10		$28.90	
6	Vegetables	$2.29	30		$68.70	
7	Chicken tings	$2.29	20		$45.80	
8			Total		$90.65	
9						
10						
11						
12						
13						

2. Input the formula for the calculation.

D3   ▼   _fx_ =(B3*C3)*E2

	A	B	C	D	E	F
1				TAX RATE:	7.50%	
2	Food item	Unit price	Quantity	Sales Tax	Line Total	
3	Beef picadillo	$2.99	15	=(B3*C3)*E2	$44.85	
4	Chipotle shrimp	$3.99	10		$39.90	
5	Carnitas	$2.89	10		$28.90	
6	Vegetables	$2.29	30		$68.70	
7	Chicken tings	$2.29	20		$45.80	
8			Total		$90.65	
9						
10						

3. Press Enter. The formula will be calculated, showing the result in the cell.

	Food item	Unit price	Quantity		TAX RATE:	7.50%
1					TAX RATE:	7.50%
2	Food item	Unit price	Quantity	Sales Tax	Line Total	
3	Beef picadillo	$2.99	15	$3.36	$44.85	
4	Chipotle shrimp	$3.99	10		$39.90	
5	Carnitas	$2.89	10		$28.90	
6	Vegetables	$2.29	30		$68.70	
7	Chicken tings	$2.29	20		$45.80	
8			Total		$90.65	
9						
10						
11						

4. Select the cell you wish to copy. The fill handle will show in the bottom-right corner.

5. Click and hold the fill handle, then drag it over the cells you want to fill.

	A	B	C	D	E
1				TAX RATE:	7.50%
2	Food item	Unit price	Quantity	Sales Tax	Line Total
3	Beef picadillo	$2.99	15	$3.36	$44.85
4	Chipotle shrimp	$3.99	10		$39.90
5	Carnitas	$2.89	10		$28.90
6	Vegetables	$2.29	30		$68.70
7	Chicken tings	$2.29	20		$45.80
8			Total		$90.65
9					
10					
11					
12					

6. Release the mouse. The formula will be copied to the chosen cells, with E2 as a constant reference, and the calculations will appear in each cell.

	A	B	C	D	E
1				TAX RATE:	7.50%
2	Food item	Unit price	Quantity	Sales Tax	Line Total
3	Beef picadillo	$2.99	15	$3.36	$44.85
4	Chipotle shrimp	$3.99	10	$2.99	$39.90
5	Carnitas	$2.89	10	$2.17	$28.90
6	Vegetables	$2.29	30	$5.15	$68.70
7	Chicken tings	$2.29	20	$3.44	$45.80
8			Total		$90.65
9					
10					
11					

Format Data for Easy Viewing

Whether you're managing expenses, recording student grades, or maintaining customer data in a homebrew CRM, data manipulation and formatting are essential. Google Sheets offers basic formatting options above your initial cell. These options are visually labeled, but for quick reference, hover over an icon to view its description and shortcut key.

Features like Print, Undo/Redo, and Font Settings/Styling operate similarly to your preferred word processor, complete with matching shortcut keys. Therefore, editing a document feels familiar.

To better illustrate the functioning, let's dive into an example. Swiftly create a list of breakfast choices for tomorrow, including ingredients, quantities, prices, and YouTube video links for preparation.

The functionality is practical, making it easy to manage information. Most of my spreadsheets adopt this format—

Google Sheets simplifies capturing, sharing, and revisiting data, serving as my structured note-taking tool.

Imagine dealing with numerous spreadsheets daily or sharing them back and forth. If someone sends you content like this, it may appear monotonous. For the provided simple example, basic formatting suffices. While it achieves the fundamentals of storing and saving information, it needs more appeal to engage with daily.

Since you consume breakfast daily, let's enhance this spreadsheet's user-friendliness with formatting. First, we'll "Freeze" the top row, allowing it to remain visible even when scrolling through extensive data. It ensures easy access to the content while keeping track of your current view.

There are two methods to freeze rows:

- Navigate to VIEW > FREEZE > 1 ROW in the menu bar to lock the top row.

- Hover over the dark grey bar at the spreadsheet's top left (until it turns into a hand) and drag it between rows 1 and 2.

Freezing the header row is my initial action when creating any new sheet.

Let's enhance the header text's visual appeal through straightforward text formatting (remember, the text formatting tools are in the toolbar, positioned just above your initial row):

- Choose and drag to highlight the cells you wish to format.

- Apply bold styling to the text.

- Increase the font size to 12pt.

- Align the entire row to the center.

- Apply a grey fill to the cells.

- Next, I'll refine the "Average Price / Serving" presentation to resemble a dollar value. Here's the initial appearance:

- Let's tidy it up using the "Format as $" button for the specific values (or the entire highlighted row).

You'll observe that the selected cells now display as dollar amounts rather than regular numbers.

- If you execute this action with the entire row/column highlighted, upcoming values will adopt the same formatting!

Now that you've familiarized yourself with inserting and formatting your data, it's time to delve into calculating sums, averages, and more from your data.

Let's enhance the header text's visual appeal through straightforward text formatting (remember, the text formatting tools are in the toolbar, positioned just above your initial row):

- Choose and drag to highlight the cells you wish to format.

Apply bold styling to the text.

- Increase the font size to 12pt.

- Align the entire row to the center.

- Apply a grey fill to the cells.

Next, I'll refine the "Average Price / Serving" presentation to resemble a dollar value. Here's the initial appearance:

- Let's tidy it up using the "Format as $" button for the specific values (or the entire highlighted row).

- You'll observe that the selected cells now display as dollar amounts rather than regular numbers.

If you execute this action with the entire row/column highlighted, upcoming values will adopt the same formatting!

Now that you've familiarized yourself with inserting and formatting your data, it's time to delve into calculating sums, averages, and more from your data.

Understanding cell content

Any data you input into a spreadsheet will be saved within a cell. These cells can encompass various information, including text, formatting, formulas, and functions.

- **Textual Content:** Cells can house textual content comprising letters, numbers, and dates.

- **Formatting Characteristics:** Cells can incorporate formatting attributes that alter the presentation of letters, numbers, and dates. For instance, percentages can be shown as 0.15 or 15%. Moreover, it's even possible to modify a cell's background color.

- **Formulas and Functions:** Cells can store formulas and functions that perform calculations on cell values. For instance, in our given example, SUM(B2:B8) computes the sum of the values in cell range B2:B8 and exhibits the total in cell B9.

How to select cells

To enter or modify cell content, choose the desired cell by clicking on it. Once selected, the cell will be encompassed by a blue box. Another way to select cells is by utilizing the arrow keys on your keyboard.

How to select a cell range

Occasionally, you may choose a broader collection of cells or a range of cells.

- Click on a cell, then drag the mouse across all the cells you wish to include in the selection. Once the desired cells are highlighted, let go of the mouse button to finalize the selection of the intended cell range.

How to insert cell content

- Pick the cell you want to work with.

- Enter the content into the chosen cell and hit the Enter key. The content will appear both in the cell and the formula bar. Alternatively, input and modify cell content directly within the formula bar.

How to delete cell content

- Choose the cell you wish to remove, then use the Delete or Backspace key on your keyboard to erase the cell's contents.

How to copy and paste cells

Copying content already in your spreadsheet and pasting it to different cells is straightforward.

Choose the cells you wish to duplicate.

- Ctrl+C (Windows) or Command+C (Mac) on your keyboard to copy the cells.

- Select the destination cell(s) for pasting. The copied cells will be highlighted with a box.

- Utilize Ctrl+V (Windows) or Command+V (Mac) to paste the cells into the chosen location.

How to cut and paste cells

In contrast to copying and pasting, which duplicates cell content, cutting and pasting transfers content between cells.

- Opt for the cells you wish to move.

- Use Ctrl+X (Windows) or Command+X (Mac) on your keyboard to cut the cells. The original cell content will persist until you paste the cells.

- Select the destination cell(s) for pasting.

- Apply Ctrl+V (Windows) or Command+V (Mac) to paste the cells.

Sometimes, you only want to copy and paste specific segments of a cell's content. For such situations, you can employ the Paste Special feature. Click Edit in the toolbar, hover over Paste Special, and choose your preferred paste option from the dropdown menu.

How to drag and drop cells

Instead of using the cut-and-paste method, you can relocate cell contents by dragging and dropping.

- Pick a cell, then place the mouse pointer over the outer edge of the blue box. The cursor will transform into a hand symbol.

- Click the mouse button while moving the cell to the preferred spot.

- Let go of the mouse button to place the cell in its new position.

How to use the fill handle

At certain moments, you might need to replicate the content of a single cell across multiple cells in your spreadsheet. Although you could copy and paste the content into each cell, this approach would consume much time. Instead, you can use the fill handle to swiftly duplicate and paste content from one cell into any other cells within the same row or column.

- Start by choosing the cell you intend to work with. A small square, the fill handle, will emerge at the lower-right corner of the cell.

- Hover the mouse cursor over the fill handle, causing it to change into a black cross.

- Click and hold the mouse button, then drag the fill handle over the cells you wish to populate. A dotted black line will encircle the cells set to be filled.

- Release the mouse button to populate the designated cells.

Share, Protect, and Move Your Data

The strength of Sheets lies in its ability to create a sense of synchronization among coworkers. Collaborative spreadsheet editing is a crucial aspect of Sheets, and Google has streamlined this process seamlessly.

Here's the process:

- Click on either FILE > SHARE or use the blue "Share" button at the top right.

- Select "advanced," then input the email addresses of those who can view or edit the spreadsheet.

- Choose additional privacy settings and confirm.

- You will encounter various options upon opening the "advanced" sharing panel.

- By default, clicking the "Share" button copies a link to the spreadsheet to your clipboard. Sharing this link with someone through messenger or email will take them to the spreadsheet. However, if you haven't invited them via email (in the email field) and chosen "Can Edit," they must request permission to make changes.

- If you wish to grant editor-level access to individuals within your organization, click the "change..." button in the "Who has Access" section and pick "On - (Your Organization Name)." (This option is available only when using Google Apps for Work.)

- Individuals are considered "In your organization" if they possess an email address and a Google account associated with your company.

- You can refer to this resource for further information on sharing and permissions. It's essential to select the appropriate permissions based on your intended audience.

Sharing Spreadsheets with Your Devices and Apps

Although Google Sheets and Drive are designed for user collaboration, it's essential to recognize that frequently, your spreadsheets are initially intended for internal use, with sharing being a secondary consideration compared to actual task completion.

Enhance your spreadsheet workflows and real-time data-sharing using these valuable add-ons:

- **Google Docs mobile apps:** The Google Sheets mobile app lets you view and edit spreadsheets, share links on the go, and add users. It is a dependable companion to the web app, though not a replacement.

- **Google Drive desktop sync:** By syncing Google Drive to your desktop, you can conveniently upload local files to your online Drive. This accessibility aids collaborators and simplifies importing files into spreadsheets and other documents.

- **Third-Party tools like Zapier:** Utilizing Zapier, you can automate tasks like adding data to spreadsheets, transferring files to Google Drive, and receiving alerts for changes in Sheets. The possibilities are extensive.

Let's continue with our spreadsheet example and illustrate how to further amplify Google Sheets' capabilities by harnessing Zapier, an integration tool.

Instead of using the "Share" button to distribute the spreadsheet to colleagues, I want to send them a Slack notification indicating the creation of the new spreadsheet.

You can accomplish this by automatically sending a message to a Slack channel through Zapier's Google Sheets Trigger and Slack Action.

Downloading Your Data

If there's a requirement to share files with external collaborators, transfer files to a different platform, or maintain backups for future reference, explore the range of data export possibilities offered by Google Sheets.

The prevalent export formats include .xls (Excel document) and .csv (comma-separated values). When in doubt about the appropriate format, opting for a .csv export is generally recommended.

Use Your Spreadsheet in Offline Mode

If you've been impressed with what you've seen but were concerned about using Sheets without an internet connection, you can put those worries aside. Google Sheets offers an "Offline Mode" that automatically synchronizes your edits with the document once you're back online.

This feature proves invaluable in scenarios where you must treat Google Sheets like a desktop application, such as during a flight or road trip.

Here's what's required:

- Google Chrome

- Google Drive Chrome Web App

- Google Drive Sync

The instructions for configuring your offline synchronization are straightforward; most of the process involves downloading and utilizing the three core components mentioned.

CHAPTER 2: MODIFYING COLUMNS, ROWS, AND CELLS

The cells in each new spreadsheet are uniformly sized by default. As you start inputting data, you can effortlessly adjust the dimensions of rows and columns to suit your data layout.

In this tutorial, you'll discover how to modify the height and width of rows and columns, along with techniques for inserting, shifting, deleting, and locking them. Additionally, you'll gain insights into wrapping and merging cells.

Working with columns, rows, and cells

The initial dimensions of each row and column in a fresh spreadsheet are uniform. However, as you start interacting with spreadsheets, you'll notice that these preset sizes might only sometimes be suitable for varying cell content.

How to modify column width

In the instance provided below, certain content in column B extends beyond the visible area. To ensure full visibility, we can adjust the width of column B.

- Position the mouse pointer over the line dividing two columns, causing the cursor to transform into a double arrow.

- Click and drag the column boundary towards the right to expand the column's width. Conversely, dragging the boundary to the left will reduce the width.

- Once content with the adjusted width suits your preference, release the mouse. Now, all cell content is entirely visible.

How to autosize a column's width

Autosizing allows you to adjust a column's width to match its content automatically.

- Position the mouse pointer over the line that separates two columns, causing the cursor to change into a double arrow.

- Double-click the mouse.

- The column's width will be modified to accommodate the content appropriately.

How to modify row height

You can increase cell height by adjusting the row's dimensions. Modifying the row height generates more room within a cell, often enhancing the visibility of its content.

- Position the mouse pointer over the line that separates two rows, prompting the cursor to become a double arrow.

- Click and then drag the row border downwards to enlarge the height. Conversely, pulling the border upwards will reduce the row's height.

- When the desired row height suits your preference, release the mouse.

How to modify all rows or columns

Instead of adjusting rows and columns individually, you can simultaneously alter the height and width of all rows and columns within a spreadsheet using the Select All button. This approach enables you to establish a consistent size for the entire spreadsheet's rows and columns. In our example, we'll ensure a uniform row height.

- Click the Select All button just below the formula bar to mark all cells in the spreadsheet.

- Position the mouse pointer over the line separating two rows, prompting the cursor to change into a double arrow.

- Click and drag the row border to make adjustments to the height.

- Release the mouse when content with the new row height across the spreadsheet.

Inserting, deleting, and moving rows and columns

Once you've worked on a spreadsheet, you might discover the need to introduce fresh columns or rows, eliminate specific rows or columns, or even relocate them to different positions within the spreadsheet.

How to insert a column

A contextual menu will emerge by right-clicking on a column header, presenting two choices for adding a column. Opt for "Insert 1 left" to include a column on the left side of the current column, or choose "Insert 1 right" to incorporate a column on the right side of the current one. It will lead to the insertion of the new column into the spreadsheet.

How to insert a row

- Click the row heading with the right mouse button. A menu will pop up, offering two choices for adding a row. Choose "Insert 1 above" to add a row above the current one, or choose "Insert 1 below" to add a row beneath the current one. The newly added row will become part of the spreadsheet.

If you need to add multiple rows simultaneously, navigate to the bottom of the spreadsheet and click on the Add button. By default, this action will append 1000 new rows to your

43

spreadsheet. However, you also have the option to specify the desired number of rows to be added in the provided text box.

How to delete a row or column

Easily removing unwanted rows or columns from your spreadsheet is a straightforward process. For illustration, we'll cover row deletion, but the same procedure applies to column removal.

- Start by picking the specific row you wish to eliminate.

- Next, right-click on the row label and select "Delete row" from the ensuing drop-down menu.

- The rows situated below the eradicated one will readjust to fill its vacancy. In our example, the removal of row 8 results in row 7 becoming the new row 7.

Distinguishing between full deletion and mere content clearance is crucial. If you seek to eliminate the content of a row or column without inducing shifts in others, take the approach of right-clicking on the label and choosing either "Clear row" or "Clear column."

How to move a row or column

Occasionally, you might find it necessary to reposition a row or column for better accessibility within your spreadsheet. To illustrate, we'll demonstrate the movement of a column, although the same technique applies to relocating a row.

- Opt for the column you intend to shift, then position your mouse pointer over the column header. The cursor will transform into a hand symbol.

- Proceed to click and drag the column to the intended location. A visual representation of the column will emerge.

- Let go of the mouse button once you're content with the new placement.

Wrapping text and merging cells

In cases where the content within a cell exceeds its display capacity, you can choose between text wrapping or cell merging as alternatives to resizing a column. Opting for text wrapping will automatically adjust the row height of a cell, enabling the content to span multiple lines. Alternatively, merging cells allows you to unite a cell with nearby empty cells, forming a larger one.

How to wrap text

- Pick the cells you wish to wrap. For instance, we'll choose the cell range C3:C10.

- Access the Text wrapping options and proceed to select the Wrap function.

- The cells will be dynamically adjusted to accommodate their content.

How to merge cells

- Choose the cells you wish to combine. For instance, in this case, we're picking the range of cells from A1 to C1.

- Click on the Merge Cells option.

- Subsequently, the chosen cells will be merged into one single cell.

To reverse the merging, click the dropdown arrow adjacent to the Merge cells button and opt for Unmerge from the dropdown menu.

Freezing rows and columns

When dealing with extensive spreadsheets, there will be occasions where you'll need specific rows or columns to remain visible consistently. It becomes essential when utilizing header cells, as the example below demonstrates. By locking rows or columns, you can scroll through your spreadsheet while keeping the header cells constantly visible.

How to freeze a row

- Identify the specific row or rows you wish to keep stationary. For this illustration, we will freeze the top two rows. Note: It's unnecessary to highlight the rows you intend to freeze.

- Open the View tab in the toolbar. Position the cursor over the Freeze option, and then pick the desired number of rows to Freeze from the dropdown menu.

- The top two rows will remain fixed as you navigate through your worksheet, ensuring they're always visible at the top, even when scrolling.

How to Freeze a Column

- Determine the column or columns you want to keep in place. For this instance, we'll freeze the leftmost column. Note: Selecting the columns you wish to freeze isn't required.

- Click on the View tab in the toolbar. Hover the cursor over the Freeze option, and then select the number of columns you want to freeze from the dropdown menu.

- The leftmost column is successfully frozen, allowing you to scroll horizontally across your worksheet while retaining a view of the frozen column on the left side.

- To remove frozen rows, go to the View tab, hover over Freeze, and choose No rows. To unfreeze columns, click View, hover over Freeze, and select No columns.

CHAPTER 3: FORMATTING CELLS

O nce you've input a substantial amount of data into a spreadsheet, it can become challenging to effortlessly observe and comprehend all the information. Formatting provides the means to personalize the appearance of your spreadsheet, enhancing its readability and comprehension.

In this tutorial, you will grasp the techniques for adjusting text size, style, and color within cells. Furthermore, you'll acquire the knowledge of aligning text, introducing borders, and applying background colors to cells.

Formatting cells

Each cell within a fresh spreadsheet starts with identical default formatting. As you commence constructing the spreadsheet, you can tailor the formatting to enhance the clarity and comprehension of your information. In our illustration, we'll employ a spreadsheet to strategize and arrange a garden plot.

How to change the font size

Adjusting the font size serves to highlight crucial cells, enhancing their readability. In our instance, we'll elevate the size of header cells to set them apart within the spreadsheet.

1. Highlight the intended cell or cells for modification.

A1:E2   ▼ | fx

	A	B	C	D	E	F
1				TAX RATE:	7.50%	
2	Food item	Unit price	Quantity	Sales Tax	Line Total	
3	Beef picadillo	$2.99	15	$3.36	$44.85	
4	Chipotle shrimp	$3.99	10	$2.99	$39.90	
5	Carnitas	$2.89	10	$2.17	$28.90	
6	Vegetables	$2.29	30	$5.15	$68.70	
7	Chicken tings	$2.29	20	$3.44	$45.80	
8			Total		$90.65	
9						
10						
11						
12						
13						
14						

2. Locate and tap on the Font Size option within the toolbar. Then, opt for the desired font size from the dropdown menu. We'll choose 14 in our illustration to amplify the text.

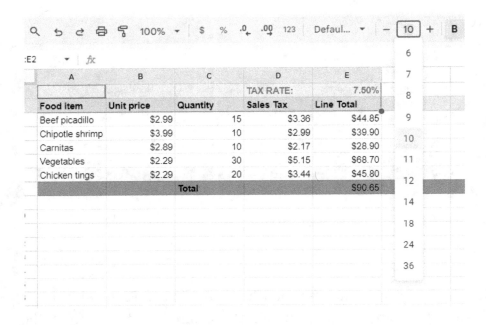

3. Observe the text transforming to the newly selected font size.

	A	B	C	D	E
1				TAX RATE:	7.50%
2	Food item	Unit price	Quantity	Sales Tax	Line Total
3	Beef picadillo	$2.99	15	$3.36	$44.85
4	Chipotle shrimp	$3.99	10	$2.99	$39.90
5	Carnitas	$2.89	10	$2.17	$28.90
6	Vegetables	$2.29	30	$5.15	$68.70
7	Chicken tings	$2.29	20	$3.44	$45.80
8			Total		$90.65
9					
10					
11					
12					
13					
14					
15					

How to alter the Font

Selecting an alternative font can further differentiate specific segments of your spreadsheet, such as header cells, from the remaining data.

1. Mark the targeted cell or cells for adjustment.

A1:E2	▾	fx				
	A	B	C	D	E	F
1				TAX RATE:	7.50%	
2	Food item	Unit price	Quantity	Sales Tax	Line Total	
3	Beef picadillo	$2.99	15	$3.36	$44.85	
4	Chipotle shrimp	$3.99	10	$2.99	$39.90	
5	Carnitas	$2.89	10	$2.17	$28.90	
6	Vegetables	$2.29	30	$5.15	$68.70	
7	Chicken tings	$2.29	20	$3.44	$45.80	
8			Total		$90.65	
9						
10						
11						
12						
13						
14						

2. Find and click on Format within the toolbar menu.

51

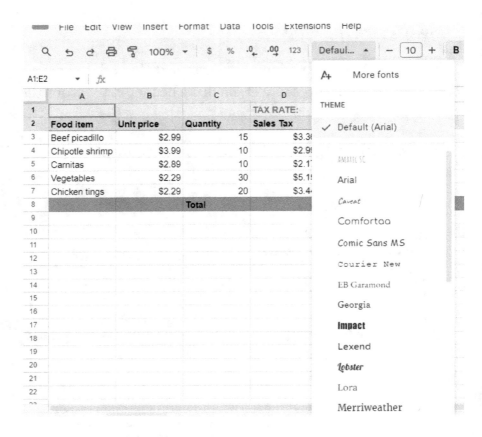

3. Hover over Font, then select a different font from the dropdown menu. In our example, we'll go with Georgia.

	A	B	C	D	E	F
1				TAX RATE:	7.50%	
2	Food item	Unit price	Quantity	Sales Tax	Line Total	
3	Beef picadillo	$2.99	15	$3.36	$44.85	
4	Chipotle shrimp	$3.99	10	$2.99	$39.90	
5	Carnitas	$2.89	10	$2.17	$28.90	
6	Vegetables	$2.29	30	$5.15	$68.70	
7	Chicken tings	$2.29	20	$3.44	$45.80	
8			Total		$90.65	
9						
10						

4. Witness the text transitioning to the newly chosen Font.

How to modify text color

1. Highlight the designated cell or cells for modification.

A1:E2   ▾   *fx*

	A	B	C	D	E	F
1				TAX RATE:	7.50%	
2	Food item	Unit price	Quantity	Sales Tax	Line Total	
3	Beef picadillo	$2.99	15	$3.36	$44.85	
4	Chipotle shrimp	$3.99	10	$2.99	$39.90	
5	Carnitas	$2.89	10	$2.17	$28.90	
6	Vegetables	$2.29	30	$5.15	$68.70	
7	Chicken tings	$2.29	20	$3.44	$45.80	
8			Total		$90.65	
9						
10						
11						
12						
13						
14						

2. Discover the Text color button within the toolbar and click on it.

53

3. A dropdown menu featuring various text colors will emerge.

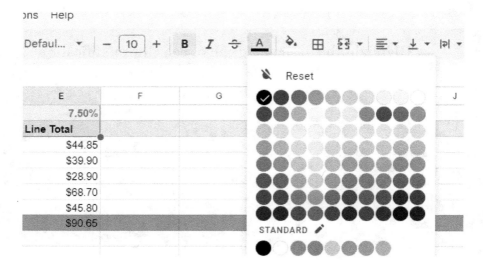

4. Pick your preferred color. In our scenario.

5. Notice the text adopting the chosen color.

How to make text bold

1. Choose the text you wish to alter.

A1:E2 ▾ | *fx*

	A	B	C	D	E	F
1				TAX RATE:	7.50%	
2	**Food item**	**Unit price**	**Quantity**	**Sales Tax**	**Line Total**	
3	Beef picadillo	$2.99	15	$3.36	$44.85	
4	Chipotle shrimp	$3.99	10	$2.99	$39.90	
5	Carnitas	$2.89	10	$2.17	$28.90	
6	Vegetables	$2.29	30	$5.15	$68.70	
7	Chicken tings	$2.29	20	$3.44	$45.80	
8			**Total**		$90.65	
9						
10						
11						
12						
13						
14						

2. Click the Bold text button for bold text, or use the keyboard shortcut Ctrl+B (Windows) or Command+B (Mac).

3. The text will transform into bold.

4. Use the keyboard shortcut Ctrl+I (Windows) or Command+I (Mac) to incorporate italics. Press Ctrl+U (Windows) or Command+U (Mac) to introduce underlining.

Text alignment

By default, any text you input into your spreadsheet will align with the lower-left corner of a cell. Numbers, on the other hand, will align with the lower-right corner. Altering the alignment of your cell content empowers you to determine the positioning of the content.

How to modify the horizontal text alignment

1. Highlight the text you intend to alter.

2. Tap the Horizontal align button on the toolbar, then choose the preferred alignment from the dropdown menu.

3. The text will adjust its alignment accordingly.

How to modify the vertical text alignment

1. Choose the text you wish to alter.

2. Click on the Vertical align button within the toolbar, and then pick the desired alignment from the dropdown menu.

3. The text will readjust its alignment.

4. Vertical and horizontal alignment settings can be applied to any cell effectively.

5. Cell borders and background colors

6. Cell borders and background colors establish clear and distinct divisions for various segments of your spreadsheet.

How to include cell borders

1. Highlight the cell or cells you want to modify.

2. Click the Borders button and select the desired border style from the dropdown menu. In our illustration, we'll select to display all cell borders.

3. The new cell borders will become visible.

How to modify the fill color

1. Changing the background color of any cell, referred to as the fill color, is a straightforward process.

2. Select the cell or cells you wish to modify.

3. Locate and click on the Fill color button in the toolbar.

4. Choose a color from the dropdown menu. In our example, we'll go with blue.

5. The new fill color will be applied.

CHAPTER 4: WORKING WITH MULTIPLE SHEETS

A Google spreadsheet has the capacity to encompass one or more sheets. When dealing with copious data, employing multiple sheets aids in organizing the spreadsheet and enhancing the efficiency of information retrieval.

Within this lesson, you will gain proficiency in generating, renaming, relocating, erasing, and duplicating sheets.

Utilizing multiple sheets

A single sheet is present upon initiating a fresh Google spreadsheet, typically labeled Sheet1. The bottom sheets toolbar exhibits a tab for each sheet you possess. You can form, alter names, remove, shift, and replicate sheets for streamlined management and navigation.

Creating a new sheet

- For instance, we will arrange the service log sheets by month. We'll generate a new sheet within the log to accommodate data for the upcoming month.

- Access the Add Sheet command on the Sheets toolbar.

- A fresh sheet will manifest within the sheets toolbar.

- Alternatively, you can introduce an additional sheet via the Insert option by choosing New Sheet from the dropdown menu.

Renaming a sheet

- Click the tab of the targeted sheet you wish to rename. Opt for Rename... from the accessible menu.

- Furnish the desired name for the sheet.

- Conclude by clicking outside the tab or pressing Enter on your keyboard. The sheet will adopt the new name.

Switching to another sheet:

- Click on the desired sheet tab in the sheets toolbar.

- The chosen sheet will become visible.

- If you aim to restrict collaborators from modifying specific sheets, you can safeguard these sheets by selecting the desired tab and clicking Protect sheet... from the emergent menu.

Moving a sheet

- Grasp and drag the tab of the sheet you intend to relocate.

- Release the mouse to position the tab at your desired location.

How to duplicate a sheet

- Tap the tab of the sheet you wish to replicate, and then pick Duplicate from the emerging menu.

- A replicated version of the sheet will materialize within the sheets toolbar, bearing a name like "Copy of May," mirroring the original sheet. If desired, you have the option to rename this Duplicate.

- For copying a sheet to another spreadsheet in Google Drive, access the sheet tab to be copied. From the visible menu, choose Copy to... Select the desired spreadsheet from the list where you want the Copy to be situated. A copy of the sheet will emerge in the designated spreadsheet.

To eliminate a sheet

- Click the tab corresponding to the sheet to be deleted.

- Opt for Delete from the displayed menu.

- A cautionary dialogue box will emerge. By clicking OK, the sheet will be eradicated.

CHAPTER 5: FORMULAS

When dealing with numerical data, Google Sheets proves valuable in performing calculations. This lesson will guide you through creating uncomplicated formulas that handle addition, subtraction, multiplication, and division operations. You'll also gain an understanding of the fundamental use of cell references within formulas.

Establishing straightforward formulas

Google Sheets presents a time-efficient advantage by enabling you to execute arithmetic operations like addition, subtraction, multiplication, and division automatically. It employs mathematical expressions referred to as formulas, simplifying these calculations. This tutorial delves into formulas involving a single mathematical operator.

Frequently, you'll employ a cell's location in the formula, known as a cell reference. The benefit of using cell references lies in their adaptability. Altering a value in a referenced cell prompts the formula to recalibrate. Utilizing cell references within formulas guarantees precision in the calculated values.

Mathematical operators

Google Sheets adheres to standard operators in its formulas: plus sign for addition (+), minus sign for subtraction (-), asterisk for multiplication (*), forward slash for division (/), and caret (^) for exponents.

All formulas necessitate commencing with an equals sign (=). It signifies that the cell embodies—or equals—the formula and its calculated output.

Using cell references

A formula that incorporates a cell's location employs a cell reference. Constructing a formula using cell references proves advantageous since it allows for effortless updates to numerical values within cells without necessitating the rewriting of the formula.

By merging a mathematical operator with cell references, Google Sheets empowers the generation of an array of uncomplicated formulas. Formulas can also combine a cell reference and a numeric value.

Formulating formulas

We'll harness simple formulas and cell references to facilitate budget calculations in our instance.

Steps for creating a formula:

1. Highlight the cell meant to display the calculated outcome.

2. Input the equals sign (=).

3. Enter the first cell address you wish to reference within the formula. It prompts a dotted border around the referenced cell.

4. Insert the desired mathematical operator, such as the addition sign (+).

5. Input the cell address of the second cell you want to reference in the formula.

6. Press Enter on your keyboard. The formula computes, and Google Sheets exhibits the result.

7. To observe the formula's recalibration, attempt modifying the value in either referenced cell. The formula promptly reflects the updated value.

8. Google Sheets might only sometimes indicate formula errors, making it imperative for you to review all your formulas meticulously.

How to create a formula using the point-and-click method:

1. Instead of manually entering cell addresses, you can click on the cells you wish to incorporate into your formula.

2. Highlight the cell designated for displaying the computed result.

3. Input the equals sign (=).

4. Click on the initial cell you intend to reference within the formula. The cell's address becomes visible within the formula.

5. Insert the desired mathematical operator for the formula, such as the multiplication sign (*).

6. Click on the second cell you wish to reference within the formula. The cell's address appears in the formula, completing the reference.

7. Press the Enter key on your keyboard. The formula will be computed, and the resultant value will materialize in the cell.

How to edit a formula

Occasionally, you might need to alter a formula already in place. In our illustration, we mistakenly entered an inaccurate cell address in our formula, necessitating a correction.

1. Double-click the cell housing the formula you wish to modify. The formula will become visible within the cell.

2. Proceed to make the necessary adjustments to the formula. In our scenario, we will substitute C4 with C5.

3. Upon completion, press the Enter key on your keyboard. The formula will recalculate, and the

updated value will emerge in the cell, showcasing the newly computed result.

Order of operations

Google Sheets follows a specific order of operations to calculate formulas: parentheses, exponentiation, multiplication and division, and addition and subtraction. A helpful mnemonic is "Please Excuse My Dear Aunt Sally" (PEMDAS). For instance, applying the order step by step is crucial when working with the formula 10+(6-3)/2^2*4-1.

Starting with parentheses: 10+(6-3)/2^2*4-1

- Evaluate the expression inside the parentheses: 6-3=3.

- Next, consider exponents: 10+3/2^2*4-1

- Address the exponent: 2^2=4.

Moving on to multiplication and division, prioritizing division: 10+3/4*4-1

- Resolve division first: 3/4=0.75.

- Continuing with multiplication and division: 10+0.754-1

- Compute multiplication: 0.754=3.

- Finally, tackle addition and subtraction from left to right: 10+3-1

- Calculate the addition: 10+3=13.

- Complete the last subtraction operation: 13-1=12.

The answer is 12. This outcome matches what you'd achieve using Excel or other spreadsheet software.

Creating complex formulas

The provided instance illustrates how Google Sheets applies the order of operations to solve intricate formulas. In the given scenario, cell D6 contains a complex formula that computes the sales tax by combining prices and multiplying them by the 5.5% tax rate (0.055).

Google Sheets adheres to the order of operations by first summing the values within the parentheses: It is multiplied by the tax rate: $274.10*0.055. Consequently, the outcome shows the tax as $15.08.

It's vital to observe the order of operations when formulating a formula; otherwise, Google Sheets might yield inaccurate outcomes. In the illustrated case, omitting the parentheses leads to incorrect results due to the first multiplication. Parentheses efficiently determine the priority of calculations within Google Sheets.

How to create a complex formula using the order of operations

In the presented example, we integrate cell references and numerical values to generate a formula that calculates the subtotal for a catering invoice. The process involves computing individual menu item costs and subsequently summing them.

Choose the cell for the formula, like cell C5 in our demonstration.

Input your formula; we'll type =B3C3+B4C4 in our instance. This formula adheres to the order of operations: it first multiplies 2.79 by 35 to get 97.65 and 2.29 by 20 to get 45.80. It then adds these results to obtain a total of 97.65+45.80.

Carefully verify the formula's accuracy and press Enter. The formula will calculate and display the result, as seen in our example, where the subtotal is $143.45.

Creating a function

Google Sheets provides a range of functions at your disposal.

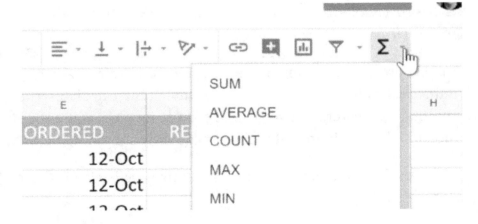

Below are several commonly used functions:

- **SUM:** This function aggregates all cell values within the provided range.

- **AVERAGE:** This function computes the mean of the values within the specified range. It adds up cell values and then divides by the count of cells in the range.

- **COUNT:** This function tallies the cells containing numeric data in the given range. It proves valuable for swift item counting within a cell range.

- **MAX:** This function identifies the greatest value among the cells in the given range.

- **MIN:** This function pinpoints the smallest value within the cells encompassed by the specified range.

How to create a function using the Functions button

The Functions button facilitates the automated retrieval of results for a cell range. The outcome is exhibited in the cell positioned beneath the range.

1. Opt for the cell range you wish to incorporate into the argument. In our illustration, we'll go with D3:D12.

f_x 52.32

	A	B	C	D
2	ITEM	QUANTITY	UNIT PRICE	LINE TOTAL
3	Tomatoes (case of 12)	3	$17.44	$52.32
4	Black Beans (case of 10)	5	$20.14	$100.70
5	All Purpose Flour (50 lb.)	5	$14.05	$70.25
6	Corn Meal/Maza (25 lb.)	5	$18.69	$93.45
7	Brown Rice (25 lb.)	5	$10.99	$54.95
8	Lime Juice (1 gallon)	5	$11.99	$59.95
9	Tomato Juice (case of 10)	3	$19.49	$58.47
10	Hot Sauce (1 gallon)	8	$7.35	$58.80
11	Salsa, Medium (1 gallon)	12	$8.47	$101.64
12	Olive Oil (2.5 gallon)	4	$28.69	$114.76
13			TOTAL	

2. Click the Functions button and select the desired function from the dropdown menu. For instance, we'll choose SUM.

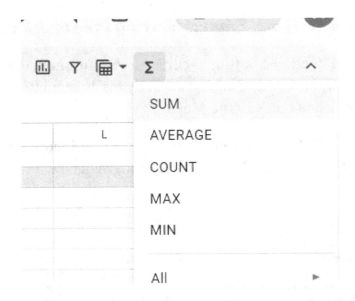

3. The chosen function is visible in the cell immediately beneath the selected cells.

fx | =SUM(D3:D12)

	A	B	C	D
2	ITEM	QUANTITY	UNIT PRICE	LINE TOTAL
3	Tomatoes (case of 12)	3	$17.44	$52.32
4	Black Beans (case of 10)	5	$20.14	$100.70
5	All Purpose Flour (50 lb.)	5	$14.05	$70.25
6	Corn Meal/Maza (25 lb.)	5	$18.69	$93.45
7	Brown Rice (25 lb.)	5	$10.99	$54.95
8	Lime Juice (1 gallon)	5	$11.99	$59.95
9	Tomato Juice (case of 10)	3	$19.49	$58.47
10	Hot Sauce (1 gallon)	8	$7.35	$58.80
11	Salsa, Medium (1 gallon)	12	$8.47	$101.64
12	Olive Oil (2.5 gallon)	4	$28.69	$114.76
13			TOTAL	=SUM(D3:D12)

4. Hit the Enter key on your keyboard. The function will be computed, and the outcome will materialize in the cell. In our example, the total of D3:D12 amounts to $765.29.

	C	D	
TITY	**UNIT PRICE**	**LINE TOTAL**	**ORD**
3	$17.44	$52.32	
5	$20.14	$100.70	
5	$14.05	$70.25	
5	$18.69	$93.45	
5	$10.99	$54.95	
5	$11.99	$59.95	
3	$19.49	$58.47	
8	$7.35	$58.80	
12	$8.47	$101.64	
4	$28.69	$114.76	
	TOTAL	**$765.29**	

How to create a function manually

Should you already be familiar with the function name, inputting it is straightforward. In the ensuing example detailing cookie sales figures, we'll employ the AVERAGE function to compute the average units sold by each troop.

1. Identify the destination cell for the result. In our case, we'll choose C10.

71

	A	B	C
1	**Frontier Kids Cookie Sales**		
2	**Troop Name**	**Troop ID**	**Units Sold**
3	North Bend	#3506	1004
4	Silver Lake	#2745	938
5	Mountain Top	#1038	745
6	Rocky Trail	#3759	729
7	Forest Path	#4157	862
8	Green Valley	#1932	890
9	River View	#4233	775
10		**Average Units**	

2. Commence with an equals sign (=), followed by the desired function name. Alternatively, you can choose the function from the list of suggested options that emerge beneath the cell during typing. For our instance, we'll type =AVERAGE.

fx =AVERAGE

	A	B	C	D
1	**Frontier Kids Cookie Sales**			
2	**Troop Name**	**Troop ID**	**Units Sold**	
3	North Bend	#3506	1004	
4	Silver Lake	#2745	938	
5	Mountain Top	#1038	745	
6	Rocky Trail	#3759	729	
7	Forest Path	#4157	862	
8	Green Valley	#1932	890	
9	River View	#4233	775	
10		**Average Units**	=AVERAGE	
11			AVERAGE	
12			Numerical average value in a dataset, ignoring text.	
13			AVERAGEA	
14			AVERAGEIF	
15			AVERAGEIFS	
16				

3. While manually entering a function, Google Sheets will exhibit a window listing the precise arguments requisite. This window emerges upon typing the initial parenthesis and persists as arguments are input.

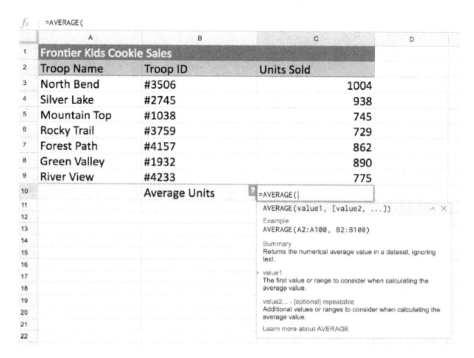

4. Within the parentheses, indicate the cell range for the argument. In our illustration, we'll input (C3:C9). This formula will sum the values in cells C3:C9 and then divide the sum by the total count of values in that range.

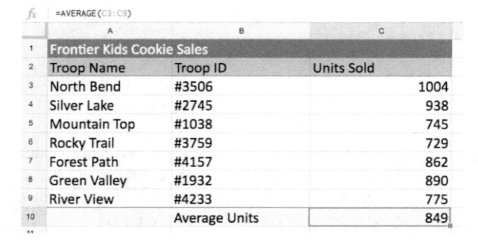

fx	=AVERAGE(C3:C9)		
	A	B	C
1	**Frontier Kids Cookie Sales**		
2	Troop Name	Troop ID	Units Sold
3	North Bend	#3506	1004
4	Silver Lake	#2745	938
5	Mountain Top	#1038	745
6	Rocky Trail	#3759	729
7	Forest Path	#4157	862
8	Green Valley	#1932	890
9	River View	#4233	775
10		Average Units	=AVERAGE(C3:C9)
11			

5. Tap the Enter key on your keyboard, and the outcome will materialize.

fx	=AVERAGE(C3:C9)		
	A	B	C
1	**Frontier Kids Cookie Sales**		
2	Troop Name	Troop ID	Units Sold
3	North Bend	#3506	1004
4	Silver Lake	#2745	938
5	Mountain Top	#1038	745
6	Rocky Trail	#3759	729
7	Forest Path	#4157	862
8	Green Valley	#1932	890
9	River View	#4233	775
10		Average Units	849
11			

Add, Average, and Filter Data with Formulas

Much like other spreadsheet applications, Google Sheets offers an array of predefined formulas tailored for various statistical and data manipulation tasks. These formulas can be combined to enhance calculations and sequence operations. If you're already adept at number crunching in Excel, you'll find that the same formulas generally apply seamlessly in Google Sheets.

Our focus here will be on the five most prevalent formulas, accessible from the formula dropdown menu in the top navigation.

You can click on a formula to insert it into a cell or start typing any formula beginning with the = sign followed by the formula's name. Sheets will automatically provide suggestions or fill-in formulas based on your input, mitigating the need to memorize them all.

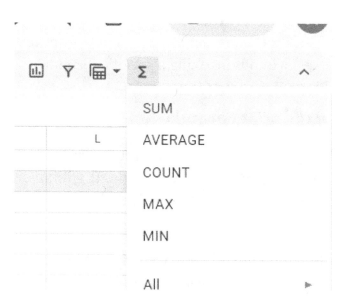

The fundamental formulas in Sheets encompass:

- **SUM:** Summates values within a cell range (e.g., 1+2+3+4+5 = sum of 15)

- **AVERAGE:** Computes the mean of a cell range (e.g., 1,2,3,4,5 = average of 3)

- **COUNT:** Tallies the values within a cell range (e.g., 1, blank,3,4,5 = 4 cells with values)

- **MAX:** Identifies the highest value in a cell range (e.g., 1,2,3,4,5 = highest is 5)

- **MIN:** Pinpoints the lowest value in a cell range (e.g., 1,2,3,4,5 = lowest is 1)

- **Basic Arithmetic:** Additionally, you can perform addition, subtraction, and multiplication directly in a cell without invoking a specific formula.

Using the SUM Formula

We'll begin by calculating the total ingredients required for each recipe using the SUM formula. It will involve adding up the values within the recipe cells to arrive at a comprehensive total.

The fundamental formulas, accessible through the top navigation, can be applied in three ways:

- Highlight a range and click the formula, resulting in the total appearing below or beside the range.

- Choose the result cell where you want the outcome, click the formula, and select the cell range for the operation.

- Manually type the formula in the result cell (including the = sign), then input or select the cell range.

- I'll illustrate all three techniques in the GIF below. Initially, I'll sum up the ingredients by selecting a range and utilizing the SUM formula from the menu. Next, I'll choose a result cell and highlight the cells for summation. Finally, I'll show how to input the formula and the cell range manually.

- Remember, to choose a cell range, click the first cell, hold SHIFT, and click the last cell in the range (e.g., A1 through A10).

- Once you've selected the cells for addition, press ENTER. A gray help section emerges as I begin typing the formula in my example. For your initial formula creation, a blue highlight and a question mark will appear next to the cell instead.

You can toggle the formula's contextual help on or off by clicking the question mark. These tips provide insights into the type of information compatible with each formula, streamlining your formula creation process, especially when combining formulas.

- Now that our SUM formula is ready to aggregate the ingredients, ensure it applies to every cell in that row. I'll select the formula cell and drag the blue dot across the adjacent cells to duplicate the formula.

- Upon copying the formula, you'll notice it adjusts the referenced cell range about the new cell. For example, in the "Scrambled Eggs" column, the range was SUM(B2:B8), but in "French Toast," it becomes SUM(C2:C8).

Using the COUNT formula

Having determined the required number of components for each recipe, I'm now interested in assessing the level of complexity involved in their preparation. For simplicity, fewer ingredients signify a less intricate recipe.

I'll employ the COUNT formula to calculate the ingredient count in each recipe.

- The COUNT formula evaluates whether cells within a range are empty or not, providing a total of filled cells.

- Setting up this formula in my spreadsheet mirrors configuring my SUM row.

Here's an additional technique we didn't cover earlier: highlight the cell range you intend to count and examine the bottom right corner of your spreadsheet. If you've highlighted a pure sequence of numbers, Sheets will automatically SUM them and display the outcome. It will COUNT the values for a mixed range of numbers and text.

- Furthermore, you can perform any of the five number-based operations on a range of numbers by clicking the SUM button at the bottom right and choosing the new default formula from the pop-out menu.

- Subsequently, every time you highlight a range, it will execute the last-selected formula.

- My spreadsheet says "Cereal" is the least complicated breakfast option. However, I still need to decide whether an easy breakfast is worth pursuing.

- What if the cost proves excessive? What if preparing another meal with extra effort saves money?

- To refine our decision, we'll ascertain the average cost per serving of the breakfast alternatives using the AVERAGE formula.

Using the AVERAGE formula

I've included simulated minimum and maximum prices per unit beside my breakfast options in the ingredients list. We aim to determine an average price for each ingredient using the low and high rates, followed by multiplying this average price by the respective unit count in each recipe.

- To initiate this process, I'll highlight the range of values, which, in this scenario, is side by side rather than in a vertical sequence. Then, I'll select the AVERAGE formula from the toolbar.

- The result will be placed adjacent to the maximum price column. Subsequently, I'll drag the formula downward to extend its application to other minimum and maximum price combinations.

- I'll assign the label "Average Unit Cost" to the column to provide clear context. Now, let's calculate the breakfast's cost using straightforward arithmetic.

Using Simple Arithmetic Formulas

We're required to compute the breakfast's overall cost by multiplying each ingredient's average price by its unit count in the recipe. To achieve this, manually input a formula into the "Avg Price" row.

Our fundamental arithmetic formula would appear as follows for the "Scrambled Eggs" column:

=$I2B2+$I3B3+$I4B4+$I5B5+$I6B6+$I7B7+$I8*B8

The $ symbol preceding the column (representing average prices) notifies Sheets that we consistently want to refer to column I regardless of where we place the formula. This way, replicating the formula for other recipes will perpetually utilize the average unit cost column. It ensures that the reference remains static, in contrast to the shifting in the SUM and COUNT instances when copying.

If you prefer to avoid manual input, there are neater approaches to performing this type of calculation. An advanced formula that achieves the same price computation is:

=SUM(ARRAY FORMULA(B2:B8*$I2:$I8))

Sheets offers numerous formulas to handle intricate tasks for you, many of which we'll delve into in subsequent chapters.

Now that we possess functional data and calculations, my colleagues, who are likely contemplating breakfast tomorrow, could benefit from this sheet.

Let's prepare to share our spreadsheet and invite collaborators to view, edit, and utilize our data.

Google Sheets function list

You can delve into the Google Sheets function list if you possess spreadsheet expertise and aim to perform more intricate calculations in Google Sheets. This compilation is a valuable resource encompassing numerous financial, statistical, and data analysis functions.

For those accustomed to the functions featured in Microsoft Excel's Function Library, you'll notice a substantial overlap with the Google Sheets function list, as it incorporates many of the same functions.

How to access the function list

Click the Functions button and choose "More functions..." from the dropdown list. This action will open the Google Sheets function list in a new browser tab.

- After mastering basic functions, consider experimenting with more advanced options such as VLOOKUP.

CHAPTER 6: SORTING AND FILTERING DATA

G oogle Sheets provides the capability to analyze and manipulate substantial volumes of data. As you augment your spreadsheet with more content, the significance of arranging the information becomes evident. Google Sheets empowers you to restructure your data through sorting and filtering. Sorting allows you to organize data alphabetically or numerically while filtering aids in narrowing down data and concealing specific portions from sight.

In this chapter, You'll grasp the techniques to sort data, enhancing the visibility and organization of your spreadsheet's contents. Additionally, you'll acquire the skills to employ data filters, enabling you to exhibit only the requisite information.

Types of sorting

When arranging data, it's crucial to determine whether you intend to apply the sorting to the entire sheet or a specific set of cells.

- "Sort sheet" arranges all data in the spreadsheet based on a single column. It ensures that related information across each row remains cohesive after the sorting. The Name column has been sorted in the illustration below, organizing client names in alphabetical order. Corresponding address details are retained alongside each name.

- On the other hand, "Sort range" arranges data within a defined cell range. It proves advantageous when handling sheets featuring multiple tables. The sorting within a range won't impact other content present on the worksheet.

How to sort a sheet

In this instance, we'll arrange a roster of customers alphabetically by their last names. To ensure accurate sorting, your worksheet should incorporate a header row to label each column. We will affix the header row, preventing its inclusion in the sorting process.

1. Access the View tab and position the cursor over Freeze. Opt for "1 row" from the ensuing menu.

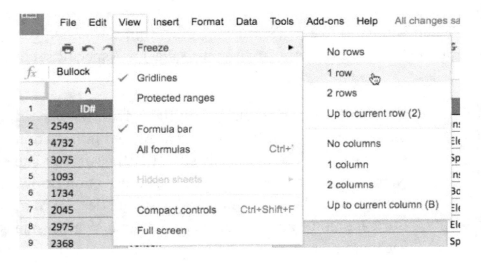

2. The header row is now secured. Determine the column for sorting, and click a cell within that column.

	A	B	C
1	ID#	Customer Last Name	Item Description
2	2045	Smith	15" Suzu Laptop
3	4732	Carter	50" LED Suzu Flat Screen TV
4	3075	Li	
5	2549	Bullock	1975 Phillip Electric Guitar
6	1734	Hernandez	
7	2975	Kokumi	
8	2368	Jensen	
9	3056	Chang	

3. Navigate to the Data tab and choose either "Sort Sheet by column, A-Z (ascending)" or "Sort Sheet by column, Z-A (descending)." In our case, we'll opt for "Sort Sheet by column, A-Z."

| File | Edit | View | Insert | Format | Data | Tools | Add-ons | Help | All ch |

🖶 ↶ ↷ 🖌 $ % .0 .00 | Sort sheet by **column B**, A → Z **B**

Sort sheet by **column B**, Z → A

Smith

Sort range...

Named ranges...

Protected sheets and ranges...

Split text to columns...

▽ Filter

Filter views...   ▶

Pivot table...

Validation...

A	B
ID#	Customer Last Na
2045	Smith
4732	Carter
3075	Li
2549	Bullock
1734	Hernandez
2975	Kokumi
2368	Jensen
3056	Chang
3856	Benner
1839	Oluwatoke

4. The sheet will be sorted as per your choice.

A	B	
ID#	**Customer Last Name**	
2376	Barnes	6 Strin
3856	Benner	1st Ed.
2549	Bullock	1975 F
1945	Bullock	
4732	Carter	50" LE
3056	Chang	
2876	Doan	
1056	Dwivedi	1950s
4790	Fisher	

How to sort a range

For example, We'll sort a supplementary table within a T-shirt order form. We aim to organize the quantity of shirts ordered based on the class.

- Highlight the cell range earmarked for sorting. In this case, we'll opt for cell range G3:H6.

- Access the Data tab and choose "Sort range" from the dropdown menu.

- The Sorting dialog box materializes. Designate the column by which you intend to sort.

- Opt for either ascending or descending order. In our case, we'll go with descending (Z-A). Subsequently, hit the Sort button.

- The specified range will be arranged in alignment with your preferences. In our scenario, the data has been sorted in descending order based on the Orders column.

How to create a filter

In our scenario, we'll implement a filter onto an equipment log spreadsheet to exclusively exhibit available laptops and projectors for checkout. Your worksheet should contain a header row that identifies the respective columns to ensure the filtering process functions accurately. We will secure the header row to prevent its inclusion in the filter.

- Access the View tab and place the cursor over Freeze. Opt for "1 row" from the menu displayed.

- Select any cell containing data.

- Click the Filter button.

- A dropdown arrow emerges within each column header.

- Select the dropdown arrow associated with the column you intend to filter. For example, we'll filter column B to showcase specific equipment types.

- Click "Clear" to eradicate all the checkboxes.

- Mark the data you wish to filter and then click OK. In our illustration, we'll tick "Laptop" and "Projector" to view these equipment types exclusively.

- The data will be filtered, temporarily concealing any content that doesn't meet the specified criteria. As demonstrated, only laptops and projectors are presently visible.

Applying multiple filters

Filters can be combined, enabling you to employ multiple filters to refine your outcomes. In this instance, we've already filtered the spreadsheet to display laptops and projectors, and now we wish to narrow the results further to showcase only the laptops and projectors that were checked out in August.

1. Access the dropdown arrow linked to the column you intend to filter. Here, we'll append a filter to column D to examine data by date.

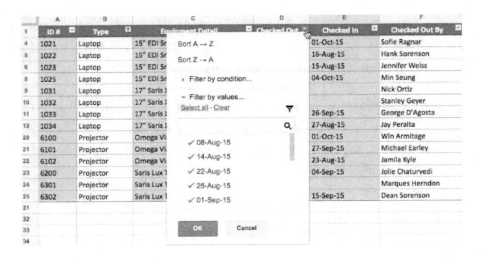

2. Tick or untick the boxes based on your desired data criteria, then click OK. In our case, we'll untick all except August.

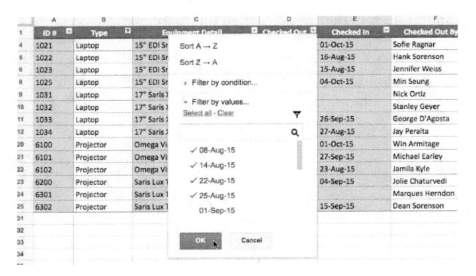

3. The new filter will be enacted. The spreadsheet is currently filtered in this example, exhibiting solely the laptops and projectors checked out in August.

	A	B	C	D	E	F
1	ID #	Type	Equipment Detail	Checked Out	Checked In	Checked Out By
5	1022	Laptop	15" EDI SmartPad L200-3 Laptop	14-Aug-15	16-Aug-15	Hank Sorenson
6	1023	Laptop	15" EDI SmartPad L200-3 Laptop	08-Aug-15	15-Aug-15	Jennifer Weiss
12	1034	Laptop	17" Saris X-10 Laptop	25-Aug-15	27-Aug-15	Jay Peralta
22	6102	Projector	Omega VisX 1.0	22-Aug-15	23-Aug-15	Jamila Kyle
31						

For collaborative efforts on a sheet, you can create a filter view. This approach permits you to filter data without impacting the perspectives of others; it solely affects your outlook. Furthermore, it enables you to label and save multiple views. To establish a filter view, click the dropdown arrow adjacent to the Filter button.

How to clear all filters

1. Select the Filter button, and the spreadsheet will revert to its initial appearance.

F	G	H
Checked Out By		
Shannon Nguyen		
Sela Shenard		

Understanding the new Google Sheets

Google Sheets represents an upgraded version and rebranding of the former Google Spreadsheets, an online spreadsheet application within Google Drive. The enhanced platform incorporates numerous fresh attributes that simplify spreadsheet creation, sharing, and editing within Google Drive. Our aim is to present a concise overview of Google Sheets and address some queries you might have regarding its functionalities.

What's new in Google Sheets?

Google Sheets closely resembles its predecessor, Google Spreadsheets, yet introduces a host of intriguing new functionalities. Here are some of the standout features that prove highly valuable and significant:

- **Offline functionality:** Google Sheets offers the capability to establish offline access within the Chrome browser. It empowers you to craft and edit Chrome spreadsheets, even offline. Upon reconnection to the Internet, Google Sheets seamlessly synchronizes and updates your work.

- **Filter views:** A distinctive trait of Google Sheets is the ability to employ filter views, which allow you to filter a shared spreadsheet without interrupting other collaborators. Furthermore, you can assign names and save multiple filter views, streamlining the process of data filtration.

- **Function assistance:** When entering formulas in Google Sheets, a pop-up dialog emerges, presenting suggestions and explanations for functions and their parameters. Supplementary information links are also provided for deeper understanding.

- **Customized number formatting:** Google Sheets enables the creation of personalized number, currency, and date formats tailored to your preference. Your custom format is stored within the number formatting dropdown menu, facilitating easy reuse.

- **Personalized conditional formatting rules:** Similar to conditional formatting in Excel or Google Spreadsheets, Google Sheets enables rules for conditional formatting based on bespoke formulas. These formulas can reference data beyond the cell being formatted.

- **Google Sheets add-ons:** While you might be acquainted with the Google Drive Add-on store, Google Sheets now boasts its own Add-on store. This resource can be accessed by selecting "Add-ons" in any Google Sheets spreadsheet and then choosing "Get Add-ons."

CHAPTER 7: UNDERSTANDING NUMBER FORMATS

What are number formats?

While engaging with a spreadsheet, it's advisable to employ suitable number formats that accurately convey the nature of your data. Number formats effectively communicate the specific data type utilized, such as percentages (%), currency ($), times, dates, and more.

Why use number formats?

Number formats serve not only to enhance the readability of your spreadsheet but also to optimize its usability. By employing a number format, you provide precise information to the spreadsheet about the nature of values within a cell. For instance, utilizing a date format conveys the input of distinct calendar dates. It facilitates improved data comprehension by the spreadsheet, promoting data consistency and accurate formula calculations.

In cases where a specific number format isn't required, the spreadsheet typically employs the automatic format as the default option. Nevertheless, the automatic format might induce minor formatting adjustments to your data.

Applying number formats

Similar to formatting methods like altering font color, applying number formats involves selecting cells and opting for the preferred style. There are two primary avenues to selecting a number format:

1. Employ one of the prompt number-formatting commands located on the toolbar.

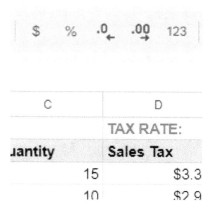

2. Explore additional choices accessible through the adjacent More Formats dropdown menu.

at Data Tools Extensions Help

| $ | % | .0← | .00→ | 123 | Defaul... ▾ | — | 10 | + | B |

✓ Automatic

Plain text

C		[
	TAX RA	
ntity	**Sales T:**	
15		
10		
10		
30		
20		

Number	1,000.12
Percent	10.12%
Scientific	1.01E+03
Accounting	$ (1,000.12)
Financial	(1,000.12)
Currency	$1,000.12
Currency rounded	$1,000
Date	9/26/2008
Time	3:59:00 PM
Date time	9/26/2008 15:59:00
Duration	24:01:00

Custom currency

Custom date and time

Custom number format

In the illustration, we've implemented the Currency format, signifying the inclusion of currency symbols ($) and depicting two decimal places for numerical entries.

			TAX RATE:	7.50%
Food item	Unit price	Quantity	Sales Tax	Line Total
Beef picadillo	$2.99	$15.00	$3.36	$44.85
Chipotle shrimp	$3.99	$10.00	$2.99	$39.90
Carnitas	$2.89	$10.00	$2.17	$28.90
Vegetables	$2.29	$30.00	$5.15	$68.70
Chicken tings	$2.29	$20.00	$3.44	$45.80
		Total		$90.65

The actual cell value can be observed in the formula bar after selecting cells featuring number formatting. The spreadsheet for formula computation and other mathematical operations harnesses this value.

			TAX RATE:
Food item	Unit price	Quantity	Sales Tax
Beef picadillo	$2.99	$15.00	$3.
Chipotle shrimp	$3.99	$10.00	$2.
Carnitas	$2.89	$10.00	$2.
Vegetables	$2.29	$30.00	$5.
Chicken tings	$2.29	$20.00	$3.
		Total	

Using number formats correctly

Number formatting extends beyond the act of cell selection and format application. Spreadsheets can autonomously apply comprehensive number formatting based on your data input method. Consequently, you must input data comprehensibly into the program and verify that the appropriate number format is assigned to these cells. To illustrate, the image below elucidates the accurate utilization of number formats for dates, percentages, and times:

- With an enhanced understanding of number formatting mechanisms, we'll delve into observing several number formats in practical use.

Percentage formats

The percentage (%) format is an immensely beneficial number formatting technique. It showcases values as percentages, like 20% or 55%, which is especially advantageous for computations involving components such as sales tax or gratuity. When a percent sign (%) is affixed to a number, the corresponding cell automatically adopts the percentage number format.

By drawing upon mathematical principles, percentages can be conveyed decimals. For instance, 15% can be expressed as 0.15, 7.5% corresponds to 0.075, 20% equates to 0.20, 55% translates to 0.55, and so forth. To explore a deeper understanding of converting percentages to decimals, our Math tutorials offer comprehensive insights.

The versatility of percentage formatting manifests in numerous scenarios. The accompanying images underscore the diverse formatting of sales tax rates in each spreadsheet (5, 5%, and 0.05):

The calculation in the leftmost spreadsheet needs to be revised due to the absence of percentage number formatting. This results in the spreadsheet misinterpreting the intent as multiplying $22.50 by 5 instead of 5%. While the rightmost spreadsheet retains functionality without percentage formatting, the central one prioritizes enhanced readability.

Date formats

When working with dates, utilizing a date format becomes essential to convey specific calendar dates, like July 15, 2016, to the spreadsheet. This format not only aids in representation but also unlocks a range of potent date functions that leverage time and date data to perform calculations.

However, spreadsheets don't interpret information in the same manner as humans. If, for instance, you input "October" into a cell, the spreadsheet won't recognize it as a date and will treat it as ordinary text. Instead, you must adhere to a recognizable format that the spreadsheet comprehends, such as month/day/year (or day/month/year based on your country's conventions). For instance, in the example below, we type 10/12/2016 to signify October 12, 2016. The spreadsheet then applies the appropriate date number format automatically.

With the data adequately formatted, many operations can be performed on this data. For instance, you could use the fill handle to extend the dates down the column, generating distinct days in each cell.

The spreadsheet has not grasped the input data if the date format isn't automatically applied. As illustrated below, typing "March 15" isn't recognized as a date, leading to the automatic format to treat the cell as text.

Conversely, typing "March 15" (omitting the "th") would be understood as a date. Lacking a year, the current year would be appended automatically to furnish complete information. Different formats like 3/15, 3/15/2016, or "March 15 2016" would still be recognized as dates.

Other date-formatting options

Click the More formats drop-down menu on the toolbar to explore additional date formatting choices. Then, select More Formats at the bottom, followed by More Date and Time Formats.

This action will unveil the Custom date and time formats dialog box, where you can choose the desired date formatting preference. These options alter the date's appearance, such as incorporating the day of the week or excluding the year.

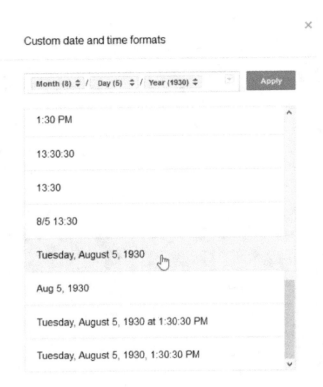

Notably, a custom date format doesn't modify the actual date within the cell; its impact is solely on how the data is presented, as evident in the formula bar.

	A	B
	f_x 2/3/2016	
1	Shipping Date	Expected Arrival Date
2	Wednesday, February 3, 2016	Wednesday, February 10, 2016
3		
4		
5		
6		
7		

Number formatting tips

Here are some useful tips to optimize your outcomes when applying number formatting:

- **Streamline number formatting for an entire column:** To manage a specific data type efficiently, like dates or percentages, consider selecting the entire column by clicking the column letter. Then, apply the desired number format. It ensures that any future data added to the column will possess the correct format, while the header row typically remains unaffected.

🖶 ↶ ↷ 🖩	$ % .0 .00 123 ▾	Arial	▾ 10 ▾ **B**

fx	Price	✓ Automatic
		Plain text

	A	B	
1	Item Name	Price	
2	Measuring Cups	$4.99	Number — 1,000.12
3	Ladel	$2.99	Percent — 10.12%
4	Slotted Spoon	$2.79	
5	12" Skillet	$14.59	Scientific — 1.01E+03
6	Garlic Press	$7.45	
7			Financial — (1,000.12)
8			Currency — $1,000.12
9			
10			Date — 9/26/2008
11			Time — 3:59:00 PM
12			
13			Date time — 9/26/2008 15:59:00
14			Duration — 24:01:00

- **Verify values post-formatting:** Applying number formatting to pre-existing data could lead to unexpected outcomes. For instance, formatting a cell with a value 5 as a percentage (%) will result in 500%, not 5%. To rectify this, you'd need to re-enter the values accurately in each cell manually.

	A	B
1	Percentage of Total	
2	500.00%	
3	7300.00%	
4	1200.00%	
5	550.00%	
6	1200.00%	
7		

- **Formula referencing with number formatting:** The spreadsheet might automatically apply the same format to the new cell if you refer to a cell with number formatting in a formula. For instance, employing a value with currency formatting in a formula will yield a calculated result adhering to the currency number format.

fx =A1/2

	A	B	C
1	$184.50	$92.25	
2			
3			
4			
5			
6			
7			

- **Maintaining original data appearance:** Opt for plain text format to preserve data precisely as entered. This format is particularly suitable for numbers you don't intend to use for calculations, such as phone numbers, zip codes, or numbers that begin with 0 (e.g., 02415). Consider applying the plain text format before entering data into these cells for optimal outcomes.

Increasing and decreasing decimals

The commands for Augmenting and Reducing decimal places offer the ability to manage the number of decimal places visible in a cell. These commands maintain the cell's value intact, focusing instead on exhibiting the value with a predetermined decimal precision.

Diminishing the decimal places will showcase the value rounded to that specific decimal point, yet the true value within the cell remains discernible in the formula bar.

However, it's important to note that the Increase/Decrease decimal places commands are ineffective with certain number formats, such as Date and Fraction.

CONCLUSION

Google's spreadsheet application has emerged as a dynamic and adaptable tool, reshaping our approach to data tasks. Its user-friendly interface, strong functionalities, and smooth interaction with other Google services position it as the preferred selection for corporations, learners, and individuals seeking to manage, scrutinize, and illustrate their data.

Throughout this guide, we've looked at the numerous functions and capacities of the spreadsheet program. Yet, the genuine prowess of this tool lies in its potential to address practical challenges and enhance efficiency. Whether you're crafting financial trackers, project management utilities, or even basic games, this application holds the potential to assist you in realizing objectives and revolutionizing your data processes.

This manual has proven to be an invaluable asset, aiding you in harnessing the complete capabilities of the spreadsheet application. Remember, the opportunities are boundless, so continue exploring and uncovering novel methodologies for handling data.

www.ingramcontent.com/pod-product-compliance
Lightning Source LLC
LaVergne TN
LVHW051708050326
832903LV00032B/4081